Generative AI for Data Privacy: Unlocking

Innovation, Protecting Rights

Table of Contents

Generative AI and Data Privacy

Part 1: Unveiling Generative AI and the Data Privacy Landscape

- Core concepts and functionalities of generative models (Gen AI for Data Privacy)
- Different types of generative AI (e.g., GANs, VAEs) and their capabilities (Gen AI in Data Privacy)
- Chapter 2: The Data Privacy Imperative
  - The importance of data privacy in the age of AI (Gen AI for Data Privacy, Gen AI in Data Privacy)
  - Existing data privacy regulations (e.g., GDPR, CCPA) and their

implications (Gen AI for Data Privacy, Gen AI in Data Privacy)

- o Challenges and considerations for data privacy with generative AI (Gen AI for Data Privacy, Gen AI in Data Privacy)

Part 2: Navigating the Privacy Risks of Generative AI

- Chapter 3: Unmasking Data Leakage and Inference Threats
  - o How generative models can reveal information from training data

- Ensuring privacy-preserving methods in synthetic data generation (Gen AI for Data Privacy, Gen AI in Data Privacy)
- Chapter 5: Deepfakes and the Looming Disinformation Threat (Optional: Consider including this chapter if the book focuses on this specific risk)
  - How generative AI can be used to create deepfakes (Gen AI for Data Privacy)

systems (Gen AI for Data Privacy, Gen AI in Data Privacy)

Part 4: The Evolving Landscape of Generative AI and Data Privacy

- Chapter 8: Regulations and Frameworks for Responsible Use

  - Potential regulatory approaches for governing generative AI (Gen AI for Data Privacy, Gen AI in Data Privacy)

  - Balancing innovation with comprehensive data privacy

protection (Gen AI for Data Privacy, Gen AI in Data Privacy)

- Chapter 9: The Future of Generative AI and Data Privacy
  - Societal and ethical considerations of generative AI (Gen AI for Data Privacy, Gen AI in Data Privacy)
  - Recommendations for responsible development and use of generative AI (Gen AI for Data Privacy, Gen AI in Data Privacy)

Part 1: Unveiling Generative AI and the Data Privacy Landscape

This part of the book dives into the world of generative AI and explores its intersection with data privacy.

Chapter 1: Demystifying Generative AI

This chapter breaks down the core concepts of generative AI, making it understandable even for those without a technical background. Here's what you'll learn:

- **Generative Models Unveiled:** We'll explore the fundamental idea behind generative models. Imagine a machine that can learn from a vast collection of images, music, or text, and then use that knowledge to create entirely new and original examples that resemble the training data. That's the essence of generative AI!

- **The Power of Different Types:** We'll delve into the various types of generative models, such as Generative Adversarial Networks (GANs) and Variational Autoencoders (VAEs). Each type has its own strengths and weaknesses, and understanding these differences is crucial for appreciating the capabilities of generative AI. For example, GANs are known for their ability to create incredibly realistic images, while VAEs excel at capturing the underlying structure of data and generating variations within that structure.

Chapter 2: The Data Privacy Imperative

This chapter shifts the focus to the critical

issue of data privacy in the age of AI.

- **Why Data Privacy Matters More Than Ever:** We'll discuss the growing importance of data privacy as AI becomes more sophisticated. As generative models rely on vast amounts of data for training, it's essential to ensure that this data is collected and used ethically and responsibly.

- **Understanding Data Privacy Regulations:** We'll break down existing data privacy regulations like the General Data Protection Regulation (GDPR) and the California Consumer Privacy Act (CCPA). These regulations define how personal data can be collected, used, and stored, and they have significant implications for the development and deployment of generative AI systems.

- **Generative AI and the Privacy Challenge:** We'll explore the specific challenges that generative AI poses to data privacy. For instance, generative models can potentially leak information about the training data they were created on, even if the data itself is not directly revealed. This chapter will discuss these challenges and pave the way for exploring solutions in later parts of the book.

By understanding both generative AI and the data privacy landscape, we can navigate this exciting and complex field responsibly.

Part 2: Generative AI and Privacy Risks

Part 2 dives into the potential privacy risks associated with generative AI. We'll explore how these models can inadvertently expose sensitive information and discuss techniques to mitigate these risks.

Chapter 3: Unmasking the Data Ghost: Leakage and Inference

This chapter tackles the spooky concept of data leakage in generative AI. Here's what you'll discover:

- **The Data Ghost Explained:** Imagine training a generative model on a dataset containing people's faces. Even if you don't directly reveal the original faces, the model might be able to learn and recreate certain characteristics, revealing information about the training data. This is data leakage, and it can be a major privacy concern.

- **Identifying Leakage Risks:** We'll explore techniques for identifying data leakage in generative models. These techniques can involve analyzing the model's outputs to see if they reveal any patterns or information about the training data.

- **Mitigating Leakage Threats:** This chapter will discuss various methods to mitigate data leakage risks. This might involve techniques like adding noise to the training data or using differential privacy, a mathematical approach that injects controlled randomness to protect sensitive information.

Chapter 4: Synthetic Data: Boon or Bane for Privacy?

Synthetic data has emerged as a potential solution to data privacy concerns. This chapter will explore the following:

- **The Advantages of Synthetic Data:** Synthetic data is artificially generated data that resembles real-world data but doesn't contain any actual personal information. This can be a valuable tool for training AI models without privacy risks associated with using real-world data.

- **The Drawbacks to Consider:** While synthetic data offers benefits, it's not without limitations. For instance, generating truly realistic synthetic data can be complex, and the models trained on such data may not perform as well as those trained on real data.

- **Privacy-Preserving Synthetic Data Generation:** We'll discuss methods for ensuring privacy is maintained during synthetic data generation. This might involve techniques like differential privacy or federated learning, where models are trained on distributed datasets without ever revealing the underlying data.

By understanding these privacy risks and mitigation strategies, we can ensure that generative AI continues to flourish while

respecting individual privacy.

Part 3: Mitigating Risks and Fostering Trust

Part 3 focuses on the exciting world of

privacy-enhancing techniques for generative

AI and emphasizes building trust with users.

Chapter 5: Privacy-Enhancing Generative AI Techniques

This chapter dives into the toolbox of techniques that can safeguard privacy while harnessing the power of generative AI. Here's what you'll explore:

- **Differential Privacy: Adding Noise for Good:** Imagine adding a little "fuzz" to your data before feeding it to a generative model. This "fuzz" is carefully controlled randomness introduced by a technique called differential privacy.

This approach ensures that the model's outputs can't be used to glean any specific information about any individual in the training data.

- **Secure Multi-Party Computation and Federated Learning: Collaboration Without Exposure:** These techniques allow multiple parties to train a generative model on their own private datasets without ever revealing the underlying data to each other. This is a powerful approach for collaborative AI development while safeguarding individual data privacy.

- **Homomorphic Encryption: Training in the Dark:** Imagine training a generative model on data that's completely encrypted! Homomorphic encryption allows you to perform computations on encrypted data without ever decrypting it. This opens doors for secure and privacy-preserving training of generative models.

Chapter 6: User Control and Transparency: Building Trust

Building trust with users is paramount for the responsible development and deployment of generative AI. This chapter explores these crucial aspects:

- **Empowering Users with Control:** Imagine having a say in how your data is used for generative AI. This chapter will discuss ways to empower users with control over their data. This could involve providing clear opt-in/opt-out mechanisms for data usage in generative model training.

- **Transparency: Shining a Light on the Process:** Generative AI models can sometimes seem like black boxes. This chapter will emphasize the importance of transparency in the development and deployment of generative AI systems. Users have the right to understand how their data is used, and developers should strive to provide clear explanations of the models' functionalities.

By implementing these privacy-enhancing techniques and fostering user trust, we can ensure that generative AI continues to thrive in a responsible and ethical manner.

Part 4: The Evolving Landscape

As generative AI continues to evolve,

navigating the legal and ethical landscape

becomes crucial. Part 4 explores these

considerations and offers a glimpse into the future.

Chapter 7: Regulations and Frameworks for Responsible Use

This chapter delves into the world of regulations and frameworks designed to guide the responsible use of generative AI. Here's what you'll discover:

- **The Rise of Generative AI Regulations:** As the potential risks of generative AI become more apparent, regulatory

bodies are starting to develop
frameworks to govern its use. This
chapter will explore potential
approaches, such as requiring
transparency in model development,
establishing data privacy safeguards,
and mitigating the misuse of generative
models for malicious purposes (e.g.,
creating deepfakes for disinformation
campaigns).

- **Balancing Innovation and Privacy:**
Striking a balance between fostering

innovation in generative AI and protecting individual privacy is a complex challenge. This chapter will discuss potential solutions, such as developing flexible regulations that allow responsible development while adapting to the ever-changing nature of generative AI technology.

Chapter 8: The Future of Generative AI and Data Privacy

The future of generative AI and data privacy is full of possibilities. This chapter explores the following:

- **Societal and Ethical Considerations:** The widespread adoption of generative AI raises important societal and ethical questions. We'll explore topics like potential biases in generative models, the impact of AI-generated content on creativity and human expression, and the ethical considerations surrounding the use of generative AI for tasks like synthetic media creation.

- **Recommendations for Responsible Development:** To ensure a bright future for generative AI, responsible development is key. This chapter will offer recommendations for developers, policymakers, and users. This might include best practices for data privacy in generative AI development, promoting transparency and user control, and fostering collaboration between different stakeholders to address the challenges and opportunities presented by this powerful technology.

By understanding the evolving regulatory landscape and considering the societal and ethical implications, we can shape the future of generative AI to be a force for good, fostering innovation while safeguarding

individual privacy.

www.ingramcontent.com/pod-product-compliance
Lightning Source LLC
LaVergne TN
LVHW051633050326
832903LV00033B/4744